Thomas Eakins

Thomas Eakins

by Lloyd Goodrich

Published for the Whitney Museum of American Art

by Praeger Publishers

New York, Washington, London

FRONTISPIECE: *ThomasEakins.* About 1901.
Photograph by Frederic J. von Rapp
Courtesy of the Philadelphia Museum of Art

Published in the United States of America in 1970
by Praeger Publishers, Inc.
111 Fourth Avenue, New York, N. Y. 10003, U. S. A.
5, Cromwell Place, London S.W. 7, England
Library of Congress Catalogue
Card Number 78-134362
Designed by Joseph Bourke Del Valle
Production supervised by Françoise J. Boas
Printed in the United States of America
Black-and-white plates by Publicity Engravers,
　printed by Plantin Press
Color plates by Lebanon Valley Offset Company, Inc.

Foreword

THIS MONOGRAPH is published on the occasion of the Thomas Eakins Retrospective Exhibition organized by the Whitney Museum of American Art in the fall of 1970.

The Whitney Museum and the author wish to express their gratitude to the many individuals and institutions who generously assisted in the preparation of the exhibition and of this publication:

To the Philadelphia Museum of Art and its Director, Evan H. Turner, who made available for the exhibition many paintings and drawings from the Museum's great collection of Eakins' works, and who assisted in many other ways.

To the Jefferson Medical College of Philadelphia, and to N. Ramsay Pennypacker, Vice President, and Oliver W. Robbins, Assistant to the Vice President, for their generosity in lending the masterpiece of Eakins' early years, *The Gross Clinic,* and two other fine portraits.

To the University of Pennsylvania and to Donald K. Angell, Vice President and Assistant to the President, for the generous loan of *The Agnew Clinic,* Eakins' major work of later years.

To The Metropolitan Museum of Art and to John K. Howat, Associate Curator in Charge of American Paintings and Sculpture, John J. McKendry, Curator of Prints, and Weston Naef, Curatorial Assistant, for their cooperation in lending from their fine representation of Eakins' works in oil, watercolor and photographs.

To the Joseph H. Hirshhorn Collection and its Curator, Abram Lerner, for lending from their outstanding collection of Eakins' works, and for many other courtesies.

To the National Gallery of Art, The Art Institute of Chicago and the Philadelphia Museum of Art for their permission to use portions of the text of the author's essay for the catalogue of the Eakins Retrospective Exhibition organized by the National Gallery in 1961, shown in the two other museums.

To the Harvard University Press and the National Gallery of Art for their cooperation in the author's forthcoming full-length publication on Eakins.

To individuals devoted to and knowledgeable about Eakins' art: the late Henri G. Marceau, former Director of the Philadelphia Museum of Art; to Seymour Adelman;

Mr. and Mrs. Daniel Dietrich; Sylvan Schendler, author of *Eakins;* Moussa Domit of the Corcoran Gallery of Art, organizer of the recent exhibition of Eakins' sculpture; Gordon Hendricks, organizer of the exhibition, "Thomas Eakins: His Photographic Works"; the Reverend John J. Shellem, Director of Libraries, Saint Charles Borromeo Seminary; Kneeland McNulty, Curator of Prints and Drawings, Philadelphia Museum of Art; and Miss Elizabeth Clare of M. Knoedler & Company.

For assistance in securing photographs in color and in black and white, to Alfred J. Wyatt and Gertrude Toomey of the Philadelphia Museum of Art; Margaret P. Nolan and Natalie Spassky of The Metropolitan Museum of Art; Elmira Bier, The Phillips Collection; Sarah Faunce, The Brooklyn Museum; Theodore E. Stebbins, Jr., Yale University Art Gallery; and Harold J. Sandak of Sandak, Inc.

The Whitney Museum wishes to thank the museums and collectors whose generosity in lending works from their collections made the Retrospective Exhibition possible:

Addison Gallery of American Art; Albright-Knox Art Gallery; Armed Forces Institute of Pathology, Washington, D. C.; The Art Institute of Chicago; Museum of Fine Arts, Boston; The Brooklyn Museum; The Cleveland Museum of Art; The Corcoran Gallery of Art; The Detroit Institute of Art; Fort Worth Art Center Museum; The Armand Hammer Foundation; Joseph H. Hirshhorn Collection and Foundation; Honolulu Academy of Arts; Jefferson Medical College of Philadelphia; Memorial Art Gallery of the University of Rochester; The Metropolitan Museum of Art; The Minneapolis Institute of Arts; National Academy of Design; National Gallery of Art, Washington, D. C.; University of Nebraska Art Galleries, Lincoln; The Newark Museum; Pennsylvania Academy of the Fine Arts; University of Pennsylvania, School of Medicine; Philadelphia Museum of Art; The Phillips Collection, Washington, D. C.; The Art Museum, Princeton University; Randolph-Macon Woman's College, Lynchburg, Va.; Reynolda House, Winston-Salem, N. C.; St. Charles Borromeo Seminary, Overbrook, Pa.; Villanova University, Villanova, Pa.; Washington University Gallery of Art, St. Louis, Mo.; The Wilmington Society of the Fine Arts; Yale University Art Gallery.

Seymour Adelman; Mr. and Mrs. James H. Beal; Mrs. Rodolphe Meyer de Schauensee; Mrs. John Randolph Garrett, Sr.; Mrs. Francis P. Garvan; Mr. and Mrs. Herbert A. Goldstone; Mr. and Mrs. Sheldon Keck; Walter Gardner Macdowell; Mrs. Thomas B. Malarkey; Mrs. Reginald Marsh; Thomas S. Pratt; Mr. and Mrs. John Hay Whitney; Harrison M. Wright; James Wyeth.

Thomas Eakins

IN THE SECOND HALF of the nineteenth century, one of the main artistic trends was naturalism. Innovating artists rejected the classic or romantic subjects of the first half of the century, and concentrated on the contemporary scene. Discarding traditional styles, they painted what they saw with their own eyes. In France the chief champion of this naturalistic viewpoint was Gustave Courbet, but it had its independent exponents in other countries. In the United States the two leading representatives of naturalism were Winslow Homer and Thomas Eakins.

Until the Civil War American painting had been predominantly romantic. The Hudson River School had pictured the wild and grandiose natural features of the continent. The genre painters had painted daily life, especially in the country, with sentiment and genial humor. The American city and the lives of city dwellers had so far found little place in established art. Even Winslow Homer had avoided the city as subject matter and devoted his art to country life—at first the summer resort and the farm, later the sea, the forest and the mountains.

Thomas Eakins' naturalism was different. He took the middle-class urban world of his place and time—Philadelphia from 1870 to 1910—and with uncompromising realism built his art out of this unromantic material. He concentrated on certain basic realities: on men and women, their faces and bodies, their clothes and houses, their work and interests. By the clarity of his vision, the strength and depth of his artistry, and the intensity of his attachment to his subjects, he gave the enduring life of art to the world in which he lived.

He was born on July 25, 1844, in Philadelphia. His ancestry was Scotch-Irish on his father's side, English and Dutch (with a strain of Quaker) on his mother's. His father was a writing master in Philadelphia schools. Thomas was the oldest child of four, and his relations to his father, mother and three sisters were unusually close. As a boy he was active in outdoor life, and grew up to be a strong youth, with a will and ideas of his own. In high school he was an exceptional student, particularly in science, mathematics and languages—subjects not often associated with a future artist. In drawing, which he took all four years, he rated 100 every year. The course consisted mostly of mechanical drawing and the study of perspective. His surviving school drawings, including some of complicated machinery, show no trace of youthful uncertainty; they are absolutely sure and precise.

His professional study of art began about 1861 at the Pennsylvania Academy of the Fine Arts. At that time the chief occupation there was drawing from casts of antique sculpture, which a student had to do for months or even years before working from the living model. Life classes were irregular, with little instruction, and most of the members drew instead of painting. The female models wore masks, to hide their identity. Eakins' life drawings, like his high school drawings, were unusually sure, completely realistic, and already revealing a strong, large sense of form.

But to Eakins this meager study of the human body was not enough. Soon after entering the Academy he began attending anatomical courses at Jefferson Medical College, including dissecting and watching operations. He continued this for several years, until his anatomical knowledge was as thorough as that of a physician, and much more complete than that of the average artist.

After four or five years of this half artistic, half scientific study, he possessed a thorough knowledge of anatomy and perspective, and was a strong draftsman, but he still had comparatively little experience of working from the living model, and practically none of painting. For more complete training he would have to go abroad. In September 1866, at the age of twenty-two, he sailed for France. Paris was not yet the Mecca for American art students, and in going there instead of to Rome, Düsseldorf or Munich, he was ahead of his time.

In these last years of the Second Empire, the Parisian art world was predominantly conservative. Eakins enrolled in the official Ecole des Beaux-Arts, choosing for his master the leading academic teacher, Jean Léon Gérôme. The foundation of the Beaux-Arts system was study of the nude—a limited discipline, but thorough. Its chief deficiency was that it was based on draftsmanship more than painting, and that the painting technique it did teach was the tight, frigid style of the academic Salons, as exemplified in Gérôme's own work. For a broader knowledge of the resources of the oil medium, or the technique of the old masters, a student would have to look beyond the school.

In March 1867, when he was almost twenty-three, Eakins was finally allowed to paint—practically the first time he had done so. (Winslow Homer, beginning as an illustrator, with little formal training compared to Eakins, did not paint regularly until he was twenty-six.) After a few months he rented a studio, to paint independently as well as in class. In the next two years of intense application he practically taught himself how to handle the unfamiliar problems of color, light and the oil medium. "For a long time," he wrote his father, "I did not hardly sleep at nights, but dreamed all the time about color and forms." But finally he could report, "I am learning to make solid, heavy work."

Judging by his many long letters home, he gave little thought to purely aesthetic matters. His viewpoint was strictly naturalistic: the painter must be faithful to nature—but nature seen largely, not imitated but re-created. "The big artist," he wrote, "does not sit down monkey-like and copy." His own painting problems interested him more

John Biglin in a Single Scull
1874. Oil. 24 5/16 x 16
Yale University Art Gallery

than the art of others. In America he had had few opportunities to see great paintings; and even in Paris his visits to the Louvre seem to have been infrequent. On the other hand, he attended the Salons regularly, making notes on the painters he liked. Almost all of them were academic: Regnault, Fortuny, Bonnat, and of course Gérôme.

But for the typical Salon nude, like those of Bouguereau or Cabanal, he had nothing but contempt. "Pictures of naked women," he wrote, "standing, sitting, lying down, flying, dancing, doing nothing. . . . The French court has become very decent since Eugénie had figleaves put on all the statues in the Garden of the Tuileries. When a man paints a naked woman he gives her less than poor Nature did. I can conceive of few circumstances wherein I would have to paint a woman naked, but if I did I would not mutilate her for double the money. She is the most beautiful thing there is—except a naked man, but I never yet saw a study of one exhibited. It would be a godsend to see a fine man painted in a studio with bare walls. . . . I hate affectation."

Of the non-academic, creative French art of those days he showed little awareness. It has been suggested that he must have seen Courbet's work in Paris, but there is no evidence for this; he left no notes on him. Courbet was the arch-revolutionist of the period, the most violent antagonist of the academic establishment of which Eakins was a part. Even when Courbet and Manet, rejected at the Universal Exposition of 1867, exhibited in a shed outside the grounds, Eakins' letters about the Exposition did not mention them, devoting most space to the machinery, particularly the big American locomotive, "by far the finest there."

AFTER THREE YEARS in Paris, in the fall of 1869, he wrote his father: "I feel now that my school days are at last over. . . . What I have learned I could not have learned at home." But before coming home he went to Spain. In Madrid most of his time was spent in the Prado. "I have seen big painting here," he wrote. "When I had looked at all the paintings by all the masters I had known I could not help saying to myself all the time, it's very pretty but it's not all yet. It ought to be better, but now I have seen what I always thought ought to have been done and what did not seem to me impossible. O what a satisfaction it gave me to see the good Spanish work so good so strong so reasonable so free from every affectation. It stands out like nature itself. . . . I have seen the big work every day and I will never forget it."

Eakins was one of the first Americans of his generation to encounter Spanish art in its native habitat, the only place it could be seen in depth. The profound impression it made on him is recorded in a notebook he kept (mostly in French) of his visits to the Prado. His great discovery was of course Velázquez. Of all the old masters, the Spaniard's naturalism and love of character more than ideal beauty were closest to his own viewpoint. Velázquez' mastery of light and its effect on color, the depth and richness of his technique, and his command of the brush, must have been the answer to the problems with which the young artist had been struggling. Of a figure in *Las Hilanderas* he wrote: "*Le plus beau morceau de peinture que j'ai vu de ma vie.*" At the same time, Velázquez' fundamental austerity—his simplification, his deliberately limited palette, and his consummate use of blacks and grays and earth tones—coincided with Eakins' temperament. Throughout his life, his art was to reveal an affinity to Velázquez more than any other master.

His second discovery was the somber naturalist Ribera. In less fundamental ways Eakins' later style was to be close to Ribera's: in his interest in anatomy and his dark color. To the other schools so fully represented in the Prado he paid less attention. He detested Rubens, calling him "the nastiest most vulgar noisy painter that ever lived." It is revealing that between Rubens, the master of the baroque and of plastic movement, and Velázquez, the austere, relatively static naturalist, he chose the latter. There were no notes on El Greco, not yet much represented in the Prado; his reaction would probably have been the same as to Rubens.

In the Prado he came to realize the limitations of the Beaux-Arts technique as taught by Gérôme—direct, opaque painting, by contrast with the richer, more complex methods of the seventeenth century. "*Il faut me décider de ne jamais peindre de la façon du patron,*" he wrote. "*Il est loin de peindre comme les Ribera et les Velásquez.*" Study of these masters had revealed to him the traditional technique of successive paintings and glazes— "*la seule manière à mon avis qui puisse donner la delicatesse et la force en même temps. . . . C'est là toujours que m'ont portés mes propres instincts.*" His own independent technical struggles were now confirmed.

From Madrid he journeyed south to Seville, where he spent the winter and spring. Here he started his first original composition, *A Street Scene in Seville*. It caused him all kinds of trouble, and he wrote that it "will be an ordinary sort of picture, with good things here and there, so that a painter can see it is at least earnest clumsiness"—too modest a statement, for it reveals a strong personal vision.

After six months in Spain he returned to Paris, and sailed for home in time to arrive in Philadelphia for the Fourth of July, 1870. He was never to leave America again.

FEW MAJOR ARTISTS have been so closely identified with a particular community as Eakins. Except for his four years abroad and a few trips within the United States, his entire life was spent in Philadelphia—almost all of it in the same house, at 1729 Mount Vernon Street, to which the family had moved when he was a young child, and where he was to live the rest of his days.

Most young American artists returning from abroad in the post-Civil-War years found the native scene raw and ugly, and hard to assimilate into art. But Eakins was of stronger fibre. He immediately began painting the world he had known before he went to Paris. He had retained his youthful love of outdoor activities, and they supplied subjects for many of his first pictures. Rowing on the Schuylkill River was a popular Philadelphia sport, which he himself enjoyed, and which provided opportunities to see the human body in action. A number of his early paintings and watercolors were of rowers racing or practising. Then there were sailboat races on the Delaware, and hunting for plover and reed-birds in the New Jersey marshes across the river.

These were all virgin themes. Every subject was part of his daily life, every figure a portrait of someone he knew, every scene a familiar one. It was the material closest to him, presented with utter fidelity to facts. There was no sign of a derived style: compared to French academicism, these works had vitality; nor were they Whistlerian reminiscences of Velázquez. They were products of a first-hand vision, almost photographically clear and precise. Even the light and atmosphere were those of America, not of Europe: the high remote sky, the strong sunlight, the clear air, the brown bareness of grass and trees for half the year. These were things he had not learned in Gérôme's studio or in the Prado. Here was a strong, original mind dealing directly with actualities.

While Eakins, like Winslow Homer, was devoted to outdoor life, and many of his early paintings were of outdoor activities, nature to him was not something loved for itself, as with Homer. Eakins' art was always centered on humanity, and for him nature was an environment for man and his work and recreations—a benign and health-giving environment, but not the principal actor in his pictures. Among all his finished paintings there is only one pure landscape. In his outdoor scenes there is no emphasis on nature's evanescent moods, and no emotional identification with them, as in George Inness' works. Rather, his concern was with nature's structure and forms. Outdoor light was all-important, and it was observed and recorded with the utmost precision; but it was important as the great revealer of forms, not as a phenomenon in itself.

Other early paintings were of his family, seen in the setting of their home, engaged in their everyday occupations. *The Chess Players* shows two old friends of his father playing, while the latter looks on. In *Home Scene* his sister Margaret, at the piano, turns to look down at their youngest sister Caroline, who lies on the floor drawing on a slate. These genre paintings reveal a penetrating sense of individual character, a loving care in representing familiar rooms and objects, and a reserved but deep feeling for home and family.

In these domestic scenes as in his outdoor subjects, Eakins was a complete realist. Every figure was a portrait, every object real. His viewpoint seemed completely objective, with no attempt to express subjective emotion. His purpose was to paint the world he knew best, with all possible truth and strength. And yet these works were charged with emotion—expressed not directly, but through his intimate involvement with his subjects, and the depth and power of his re-creation of them. Beauty as an end in itself was not aimed at; but these paintings achieved their own kind of austere beauty— a by-product of his search for essential realities.

AT THE SAME TIME as his outdoor and indoor genre pictures, Eakins began his long career as a portrait painter. His first subjects were his sisters and their friends, particularly the Crowell family. *Katherine* was one of two Crowell sisters; he had known her since childhood, and the year he painted her, 1872, they became engaged. It was a long engagement—ended tragically by her death. He was to remain single until he was almost forty.

Following his family portraits he launched himself as a portraitist by asking fellow Philadelphians to pose for him—people he knew and who interested him. For example, his former chemistry teacher in high school, Benjamin H. Rand, now a professor at Jefferson Medical College; and Dr. John H. Brinton, also on the Jefferson faculty. These portraits were not commissioned, and he gave them to the sitters.

A leading figure at Jefferson was Dr. Samuel D. Gross, a famous surgeon and a man of impressive appearance. Watching him in the operating amphitheater, Eakins conceived the most important composition of his early years, *The Gross Clinic*, painted in 1875, when he was thirty-one. Dr. Gross has paused in the operation, and scalpel in hand, stands talking to his students, while his assistants work on the patient. Daylight falls from above, lighting the principal actors against the dark background of students— a Rembrandt-like chiaroscuro that models the figures in strong relief. The design is pyramidal, with all its elements culminating in the magnificent head of Dr. Gross. The forms have a sculptural roundness and substance, and their relations one to another and to the space around them produce complex and powerful design. This masterpiece of Eakins' early manhood has a strength, a depth and a completeness of realization that make it one of the greatest paintings of the nineteenth century.

The subject of *The Gross Clinic* was one seldom attempted in modern art, yet of central importance in our age—the drama of science and its battle against disease. Its realism was entirely uncompromising, including the blood on the surgeon's hand. The American art world, used to the sentimentalities of the academy, reacted in predictable fashion. When the picture was submitted to the historic Centennial Exhibition in Philadelphia in 1876, it was rejected by the art jury, but Eakins succeeded in having it hung in the Medical Department of the Exhibition. Three years later it was shown by the liberal Society of American Artists in New York, and later, after an attempt to suppress it, at the Pennsylvania Academy. Some critics recognized its power, but others were horrified. One of them described it as "a picture of heroic size . . . that a society thinks it proper to hang in a room where ladies, young and old, young girls and boys and little children, are expected to be visitors. It is a picture that even strong men find it difficult to look at for long, if they can look at it at all. . . . No purpose is gained by this morbid exhibition, no lesson taught." An interesting fact, however, was the amount of space the critics gave to it. The writer quoted above, reviewing a large exhibition, saw no reason "that it was ever painted, in the first place, and that it was ever exhibited, in the second," but spoke of it first and gave more than half his review to it.

Like all his early portraits, the painting had not been a commission, and when the Jefferson Medical College bought it in 1878, the price was $200.

EAKINS WAS EXCEPTIONAL among artists in his combination of scientific and artistic interests. His medical and anatomical interests we have seen. He loved mathematics, and used to relax his mind after painting by reading logarithms and working out problems in calculus. When he came to teach, he would advise pupils to study higher mathematics, which he said were "so much like painting." "In mathematics the complicated things are reduced to simple things. So it is in painting." Pictorial perspective had always absorbed him: he wrote a long paper on it, and even a paper about the mathematical problems involved in reflections in water (the manuscripts of both are now in the Philadelphia Museum of Art).

In his early pictures, the main planes and the regular-shaped objects were constructed in perspective, based on exact measurements and mathematical calculations, like the procedure of a mechanical draftsman. This method, of course, was applied only to the parts that lent themselves to this kind of treatment, not to the figures. A perspective drawing of a rowing picture, for example, would show the shell floating on the water, the oars in exactly calculated positions, the waves and reflections carefully plotted, and the figures broadly drawn in freehand. This was the basic three-dimensional structure of the painting, which was then transferred to the canvas with transfer paper. These perspective drawings, some of which still exist, have a precise beauty of their own. Many of them were probably lost; certainly a painting like *Max Schmitt in a Single Scull,* with its fine spatial design, must have been constructed in this way.

Similar methods were followed in his large portraits. The ground-plan and the regular objects were laid out in perspective; in the case of a seated figure the floor and the chair would be constructed first. Even the signatures in his more important pictures were usually inscribed on the floor or on objects, in perspective; one such drawing shows the signature drawn flat, then projected in perspective, to be transferred to the canvas. To such lengths would he go to insure three-dimensional exactitude.

But with all his scientific interests, Eakins' science remained subordinate to his art. He was an artist absorbed in science, not a scientist practising art. His studies were closely related to painting and to specific artistic problems: the anatomical structure of the body, the dynamics of motion, the space relationships of objects. All his scientific avocations were devoted to understanding natural principles as they were involved in creating the work of art.

Beneath his scientific methods lay the deep sensuousness that is the basis of all vital art. His work speaks to us in the direct physical language of pigment, texture, color and form. It has tremendous substance—the greatest of any American painter of his time. His forms are in the full round—absolutely solid, and weighty. With all their realism, they are sculptural. There was no sense of his having to strain after these qualities; they were innate, showing even in his student life drawings. He simply felt the physical existence of things with complete, unconscious integrity.

His paintings were constructed in fully three-dimensional terms. There were no flat passages in them. The relations of forms to one another, and to the space in which they existed, arrived at by scientific perspective, were exactly understood. To the precision and justness of these relations, all his paintings, whether outdoor scenes, indoor genre or portraits, owed their strength of construction, their creation of a three-dimensional order of round forms in deep space.

While entirely naturalistic, his work differed fundamentally from the concern with mere visual appearances that marked much painting of his period. While his generation was becoming absorbed in light and atmosphere and such visual phenomena, he saw nature as solid, tangible realities. His paintings were essentially plastic: they were not merely the re-creation of things in the real world, but the creation of ordered design.

The Gross Clinic
1875. Oil. 96 x 78
Jefferson Medical College of Philadelphia

His forms were always related to the physical surface of the painting, which determines what nowadays we call the picture plane—the pictorial space in which the forms exist, within a plastic unity. There were no holes in his compositions, any more than there were flat passages.

His color from the first was dark and reserved, with prevailing grays and browns and blacks, as in the Spanish masters he admired. Earth colors predominated. Flesh tones tended to be swarthy, almost Latin. Unlike his contemporaries the impressionists, who were rivalling the brilliancy of outdoor nature, Eakins' aim was to create an equivalent to nature's tonal relations, in a lower key. To him the essential thing was not the key, but the justness of relations. He was not interested in the decorative qualities of color; what concerned him was its coordination with form. At the same time, his color in itself, within its restricted range, has a full-blooded strength and depth. Some of his paintings contain passages which in sensuous richness equal Courbet or the early work of Renoir: to cite only a few examples, *Professor Rand, The Swimming Hole, Baby at Play, A Lady with a Setter Dog, Miss Van Buren, The Concert Singer*. In such works he revealed himself as one of the most sensuous colorists of his time.

His technique, evolved by independent thinking and experimentation, assisted by study of the old masters, was more complex than that of most of his contemporaries. Painters like Sargent, Chase and Duveneck had abandoned the methods of the old masters in favor of direct painting in more or less opaque pigment, *au premier coup*. Eakins' procedure was to lay the composition in broadly in thin color, then to build it up in successive overpaintings and glazes, with the light areas and solid forms painted most heavily, the shadows and recessions more translucently. The result was a solidity and depth that could not be achieved by direct painting.

While he often made oil sketches outdoors, his finished paintings were done in his studio. Sometimes small wax models were made of figures, such as the horses in *The Fairman Rogers Four-in-hand*. Strangely enough, although he was a strong draftsman, he drew little, aside from his perspective drawings. Instead of preliminary drawings, he made small oil studies in full color, just of the main masses; these studies were then squared off and enlarged on to the canvas. Even for his watercolors, of which he painted about twenty-five (mostly in the 1870's and 1880's) his sketches were in oil—a curious reversal of the usual procedure. While a sure, relatively fast executant, he worked a long time on his larger, more complex paintings: as an extreme example, *The Concert Singer* took him two years. Lack of patience on the part of some sitters left a number of pictures unfinished, as did his habit of abandoning a painting if he was not satisfied, and starting a second version. But these unfinished works and his sketches reveal qualities of visual freshness, breadth and freedom that were sometimes lost in the finished pictures.

EAKINS' STYLE from the very first revealed little influence from other art. The naturalistic viewpoint and the artistic tastes expressed in his notebooks and his letters from abroad remained substantially unchanged throughout his life, though broadened. He retained his respect for certain French academicians: above all, Gérôme. His temporary differences with his master were forgotten and were replaced by lifelong devotion to him as a teacher and an artist—"the greatest painter of the nineteenth century," he often said. Yet it is hard to detect in Eakins' first-hand naturalism any fundamental relation to Gérôme's cold, meticulous neo-classic anecdotes and travelogues. Whatever resemblances there were between Eakins' style and that of the French academy were on the surface, whereas the differences were basic; his art had a vitality, a structural power and a plastic sense that official French art conspicuously lacked.

In mature years Eakins came to appreciate the French independents as he had not in Paris, especially Millet, Corot, Barye, Courbet, Manet and Degas. Of all these, his work was closest to Courbet's; but there is no evidence in his recorded opinions that he ranked the master of naturalism higher than the others. With all their affinities, there were deep dissimilarities. Courbet was actually not as strict a naturalist as Eakins; he was a child of romanticism in rebellion against his parentage, and there were romantic survivals in his style that could not have been to Eakins' taste.

Eakins' admirations in the past were almost entirely for the naturalists—except for the Greek sculptors, especially Phidias, who held a special place in his estimation. He continued to revere above all the Spaniards, Velázquez and next to him Ribera, who he said had succeeded best in the kind of painting he believed in. On a par with them was Rembrandt. These three were the painters to whom he referred most often in his teaching, together with the Greeks, and Gérôme. When he visited the Metropolitan Museum he spent most time with the Greek casts, and with Velázquez and Rembrandt.

There are interesting parallels between his style and that of Velázquez, especially in portraiture. *The Thinker*, for example, is close to the portrait of Pablo de Valladolid in the Prado, not only in its whole concept but in its actual color harmony. But there was a distinction between his relation to Velázquez and that of Whistler, who adapted the master's decorative qualities but not his naturalism. With Eakins the affinity was deeper: a direct relation to the realities of their respective times and countries, a grasp of character, a command of three-dimensional space, and a monumental sense of design. The example of Velázquez confirmed Eakins' innate disposition to picture his own world in his own way.

The relation to Rembrandt was similar. In Eakins' portraits and indoor genre the handling of light, particularly in modelling the most highly lighted forms such as heads, obviously owed something to study of the Dutch master. And a few rather atypical portraits such as those of F. L. Schenck can be called consciously Rembrandtesque in their subdued but dramatic light, softened edges, and deep mellow browns.

Eakins' tastes in art were never very wide or sophisticated. But they were independently arrived at, and stubbornly held. His primary interest in the art of others was in their technical rather than their aesthetic qualities, in what they could teach him—the attitude of a creator rather than that of an appreciator. His style revealed nothing like the influence of Corot on Inness, of Millet on Hunt, or of the Venetians and Delacroix on LaFarge. Unquestionably he learned much from certain naturalistic painters of the past and of his own time; but the more fundamental fact is that his art had an exception-

William Rush Carving His Allegorical Figure of the Schuylkill River
1877. Oil. 20⅛ x 26½
Philadelphia Museum of Art

ally close relation to reality, and was the product of deep, thorough study of natural forms, more than of other art.

TO EAKINS, as to most of the old masters, the human figure was the central element of art. With all his anatomical science, there was nothing coldly academic in his attitude toward the human body. His painting of it had a vitality that made him the strongest figure painter of his time in America. As a teacher his whole system was founded on study of the nude. And yet he seldom painted it. There was a deep conflict between his interest in the nude and his realism. As an artist, the body and its plastic possibilities were fundamental to him. But as a realist, he was interested primarily in picturing what he saw in the life around him; and Philadelphia in the late nineteenth century was not Greece. Only the male bodies of athletes were on public view, in sports like rowing and prize-fighting. The female form was effectually concealed beneath voluminous skirts, bustles, leg-of-mutton sleeves, and high collars. Eakins seldom gave free rein to fantasy; like Courbet, who said he would paint angels if anyone showed him one, Eakins would paint the unclothed figure if he saw it in the real world—otherwise, only rarely. (Remember his words as a student in Paris: "I can conceive of few circumstances wherein I would have to paint a woman naked.") He even objected to using professional models, finding a lack of reality in them. Many times he asked women sitting for portraits if they would pose nude for him—a habit that caused considerable scandal in the Philadelphia of those days.

Among his few paintings of the female nude were his various versions of the William Rush story. Rush, one of the earliest native American sculptors, and a Philadelphian, about 1809 had carved an allegorical fountain figure for the city water-works—a nymph in a clinging Grecian robe. As his model, a young Philadelphia belle had consented to pose. Although her posing at all was advanced for her day, there is no evidence that she did so in the nude. It is significant that Eakins chose to represent her as doing so.

This theme, so close to his own problems, appealed to him so strongly that he painted it no less than four times: early in his career, in the delightful picture dated 1877, now in the Philadelphia Museum, and another preliminary version; and twice in his old age, in 1908. That he came to consciously identify himself with Rush is shown by the fact that in one of the late versions he substituted for the sculptor's figure his own, handing the model down from the stand as if she were a queen. A strange and revealing obsession! His deep and healthy paganism, repressed by the prudery of his time and place—combined with his own strict realism—was expressing itself in this peculiarly round-about manner.

That this prevailing prudery had its effect even when he did paint the nude is suggested by the fact that almost all his nudes, both female and male, have their backs turned to us. But in the late Rush painting in which he himself appears as the sculptor, the model is for the first time turned fully towards us. In old age, he had finally freed himself from his self-imposed taboo.

EAKINS WAS a born teacher. When the Pennsylvania Academy opened its new building on North Broad Street in 1876 he volunteered to take over the life classes. In a few years he became virtual head of the school, and in 1882 he was appointed director. Most American art schools were still as backward as in his own student days: everything based on antique casts, with little work from the living model.

Eakins reversed this. Not that he objected to Greek sculpture—on the contrary, it was one of his greatest admirations, as we have seen—but to drawing from casts as a way of learning to paint. As he put it: "The Greeks did not study the antique; the *Theseus* and *Illysus* and the draped figures in the Parthenon pediment were modelled from life undoubtedly. And nature is just as varied and just as beautiful in our day as she was in the time of Phidias."

Study of the nude was made the basis of his system. Anatomy was stressed, with a dissecting-room in the school, and lectures by a surgeon as well as by himself. Animal anatomy was also studied; live horses were used as models, and even cows. He gave lectures on perspective. Students were urged to think always of the third dimension, and of the solidity and weight of the figure. In the life classes, he started them painting from the first, without preliminary drawing. "A student should learn to draw with color," he said. "There are no lines in nature; . . . there are only form and color. The least important, the most changeable, the most difficult thing to catch about a figure is the outline."

Purely artistic principles received little attention in his teaching. While recognizing their importance, he did not believe that they could be taught; the most that a school could do was to provide thorough naturalistic training. But actually his teaching had deep if not consciously expressed artistic content: its insistence on form, so unusual in America at this time. Within a few years the Academy school had become the most popular in the country, and he had played a part in changing the direction of American art education.

OUT OF HIS TEACHING came his involvement in sculpture. At the Ecole des Beaux-Arts he had studied the medium briefly under Augustin Alexandre Dumont, not so much for itself as to supplement painting. Similarly at the Pennsylvania Academy, sculpture was stressed; even the painters were required to give some time to it, and if they began to paint flat they were sent to the modeling class.

On several occasions he had used sculpture in planning his own paintings. For the early *William Rush* he made five small models of the chief figures and objects, and for *The Fairman Rogers Four-in-hand*, models of the four horses. Then in the early 1880's he became interested in sculpture as a medium in itself: particularly relief, on which he prepared a paper, the manuscript of which still exists (at the Philadelphia Museum of Art), bearing a note: "I believe this paper to be entirely original." "Relief," he wrote, "holds a place between a painting or drawing on a flat surface and a piece of full sculpture," and he proceeded to analyze the principles governing projection and recession, as logically as in his perspective lectures.

His first independent sculptures were two oval reliefs of women in old-fashioned dresses, spinning and knitting. They were commissioned by a wealthy Philadelphia art patron, James P. Scott, to be carved in stone as ornaments for a chimney-piece in his luxurious new house. But after seeing the plasters Mr. Scott refused not only to have them carved but to pay Eakins in full for the work he had done.

Undeterred by this, in 1883 Eakins modelled (probably for his own pleasure) a relief, *Arcadia,* showing a group of idyllic figures listening to a nude youth playing the pipes, and also two similar single figures. Here was a new kind of subject, paralleled by several paintings of the same time.

AMONG EAKINS' many interests was photography. As early as 1880 he had a four-by-five-inch camera, and was using it constantly. Many of his subjects, as in his early paintings, were of his family, especially his sister Frances (Mrs. William J. Crowell) and her numerous sons and daughters, at their farm in Avondale, Chester County, where he was a frequent visitor. His students figured in many photographs, the men often shown nude outdoors. There were direct links between these subjects and his Arcadian sculptures, and certain idyllic paintings of the early 1880's—of which more later. Photographs exist of the actual scene of the painting *The Swimming Hole,* with naked youths bathing, though not in the exact positions of the oil. But in a few other cases the photographed figures were copied literally; for example, in the painting *Arcadia,* the nude young man and boy are identical with photographs, not only in pose but in the precise lights and shadows. The watercolor *Drawing the Seine* is a detail-by-detail copy of a photograph, though one would not suspect this without seeing the latter; the watercolor has none of the deadness that results from some artists' use of photographs. Eakins evidently looked upon the camera as another tool for gathering visual data.

More often, however, the relation between the two mediums was more general; the photograph, while obviously a form of study for the painting, was not actually copied. Most of his photographic portraits were parallel studies of the sitter. And many were entirely independent of any painted portraits. The best of them show the same revealing sense of character, the same command of light, and even the same psychological penetration.

Eakins' photographs, which extended over many years, and of which several hundred have been preserved, rank him among the foremost pioneer photographers of his time in America. This aspect of his art, the extent of which was first revealed by Gordon Hendricks in his complete and scholarly exhibition at the Pennsylvania Academy in 1969, indicates that the camera played a larger part in Eakins' work than in that of any other nineteenth-century American painter.

He also used photography for more purely scientific purposes. The processes of human and animal locomotion were of particular interest to him. In 1884 and 1885, in collaboration with the professional photographer Eadweard Muybridge, and under the auspices of the University of Pennsylvania, he carried on a series of experiments in photographing horses in motion, and naked men walking, running, jumping, pole-vaulting, swinging weights, and throwing baseballs. Muybridge's system, a battery of cameras set up alongside a track and set off in sequence, seemed scientifically inaccurate to Eakins, so he adapted the apparatus of the French physiologist E. J. Marey, a single camera with two revolving disks pierced with openings—essentially the principle of the modern motion picture camera. Since the viewpoint remained the same and the time intervals were exactly regulated, the successive images, taken on one plate, could be compared with mathematical accuracy.

His interest in equine anatomy always remained strong, and in 1894 he produced the only writing ever published under his name, "The Differential Action of Certain Muscles Passing More than One Joint," a paper on the muscular mechanism of the horse, which appeared in the *Proceedings* of the Philadelphia Academy of Natural Sciences. The conclusion brought the subject back into his own field: "On the lines of the mighty and simple strains dominating the movement, and felt intuitively and studied out by him, the master artist groups, with full intention, his muscular forms. No detail contradicts. His men and animals live. Such is the work of three or four modern artists. Such was the work of many an old Greek sculptor."

IN MANY WAYS Eakins' life was expanding in the early 1880's. When his younger fellow artists began to return from study in Paris or Munich they came into conflict with the older conservatives in the National Academy of Design, and started the revolt that came to be called "The New Movement"—the first such in American art. This led to the founding of the liberal Society of American Artists, with which Eakins exhibited from the first, and of which he became a member in 1880—his only art organization for many years. His work was now shown fairly regularly in the big national exhibitions, and he was generally regarded as one of the leaders of "The New Movement." (All this, however, did not mean financial success; at the age of thirty-six he had sold only eight pictures, for a total of a little more than $2,000. Fortunately, he had his father's small but steady income to fall back on, aside from his salary as a teacher.)

In his fortieth year, 1884, Eakins married Susan Hannah Macdowell, a painter and a former pupil—one of his most talented, and a fine painter in her own right. Sharing completely in his interests, she gave him the constant support of her understanding and faith. Their home remained the Mount Vernon Street house. Although they had no children, the house was always full of nieces and nephews. They lived with the utmost simplicity. Eakins had no desire to go abroad again, saying that his favorite places in the world were Philadelphia and Spain. There was nothing of the recluse in him, as in Homer and Ryder; he had a gift for friendship, and he and Mrs. Eakins had a wide circle of friends. Some were artists and musicians, but others were outside the arts—scientists, physicians, professors of the University of Pennsylvania. He was fond of music, and since Mrs. Eakins was a pianist (she appears in *The Pathetic Song*, painted before their marriage), there were frequent evenings of music in their home. Eakins said that he liked to *see* musicians play and sing, and his enjoyment of the visual side of music was embodied in many paintings. His active outdoor life continued; he enjoyed boating and bathing, and he liked horses and riding (a preference that played a considerable role in his art).

He had unusually close relations with his students, some of whom remained his friends throughout his life. Many of his portraits were of them. They helped him with extra-curricular activities such as his experiments in photographing motion. His demonstrator of anatomy, J. Laurie Wallace, posed for *The Crucifixion,* strapped to a cross out-of-doors. They went on outdoor excursions with him. Eakins was always entirely natural about nudity, and preferred bathing without benefit of bathing-suits. Out of these experiences came *The Swimming Hole,* showing a group of naked men and boys, including his pupils and friends and himself—and his dog Harry—swimming in a secluded spot. In none of his previous outdoor compositions had the forms been so sculptural, filling the pictorial space amply, and flowing in controlled rhythms to culminate in the standing figure, the apex of the pyramid. This was one of his most fully realized designs, with qualities of form and movement suggesting a work of the early Renaissance.

In these years, the early 1880's, he also essayed several Arcadian subjects: idyllic figures, nude or in classical robes, outdoors in the sunlight. Here was an imaginative kind of subject quite different from his realistic outdoor scenes—an openly poetic strain. It was linked to his love of the human body, and to life in the open air; to his admiration of the Greeks; to the whole bent of his teaching. It had appeared in his photography, and in his sculpture. One can only speculate on what might have resulted if this idyllic, pagan trend had continued.

In his early forties Eakins occupied a prominent but somewhat paradoxical position in American art. His work was not popular, and some of it had met with hostility. But his realistic power could not be gainsaid, and he was recognized as the leader of a new naturalism. And he was widely known as an innovating teacher and the head of the Pennsylvania Academy school.

BUT BENEATH the surface, opposition was growing. To the conservative businessmen directors of the Academy he was still a radical. Half the students were women, of whom a conventional minority disapproved of his methods, especially his emphasis on the nude. As one of them wrote in a long, hysterical letter to the president of the Academy: "Would you be willing to take a young daughter of your own into the Academy Life Class, to the study of the *nude figure* of a woman . . .?" The crisis came in 1886, when in explaining to the women's life class the action of the pelvis in a male model, he removed the loin-cloth. As he said later in a letter to another school: "In lecturing upon the pelvis, which is in an artistic sense the very basis of the movement and balance of the figure, I should use the nude model. . . . I am sure that the study of anatomy is not going to benefit any grown person who is not willing to see or be seen seeing the naked figure, and my lectures are only for serious students wishing to become painters or sculptors."

The Academy directors told him that he must be more modest, or resign. He replied that he would remain only on condition that he was not hampered in his teach-

The Swimming Hole
1883. Oil. 27 x 36
Fort Worth Art Center Museum

ing, and the directors accepted his resignation. But most of the students, including practically all the men, sided with him. A protest meeting was held, and petitions were signed by a majority of the students. When the directors rejected them, a considerable number of the male students seceded, and founded the Art Students' League of Philadelphia, a cooperative body run entirely by the students, with Eakins as its head. Its prospectus stated that "the basis of study is the nude human figure." He did all the teaching, refusing to accept any salary.

At the League he could give his students more personal attention, and his relations with them were even closer than at the Academy. Out of the League grew one of his closest friendships, with the future sculptor Samuel Murray, who worked as his painting assistant, and at the same time learned from him the craft of sculpture. Murray became like a son to Eakins, sharing his studio for more than ten years. In turn Murray stimulated the older artist's activities in sculpture. In 1891 their mutual friend William R. O'Donovan secured a commission for two life-sized bronze equestrian statues of Lincoln and Grant, in high relief, for the Memorial Arch in Prospect Park, Brooklyn. Knowing Eakins' familiarity with equine anatomy, O'Donovan arranged for him to do the horses. The result was two of the most powerful animal figures in American sculpture, which dwarf O'Donovan's over-literal figures of the riders.

Two years later came Eakins' largest independent sculptures, two reliefs for the Battle Monument in Trenton, New Jersey: *The American Army Crossing the Delaware* and *The Battle of Trenton*. Again the commission came through O'Donovan, who executed the chief figures on the monument; but this time Eakins had a freer hand, and the two bronzes were not only faithful to historical facts (by contrast with Leutze's *Washington Crossing the Delaware*) but his most complex and fully realized sculptures.

Except for his small models for paintings, and a series of purely anatomical pieces, all Eakins' sculptures were in relief—but sometimes, as in the two horses, in very high relief, almost in the round. In a sense his sculpture was that of a painter. But seen as a whole (as it was in the exhibition organized by Moussa Domit in 1969 for the Corcoran Gallery of Art) his sculpture reveals plastic qualities as strong as in his paintings, and makes one regret that he did not have more opportunities to realize his ability as a sculptor.

The Art Students' League of Philadelphia, without financial backing, lasted only six years. In the meantime, Eakins lectured on anatomy at schools in other cities; but on several occasions his insistence on the complete nude caused the same conflict, and his courses were discontinued. So his teaching career, to which he had given so much time and energy, ended when he was about fifty.

IN SPITE of his students' loyalty, the break with the Pennsylvania Academy was a severe blow. It injured him not only as a teacher but as an artist and a member of his community. Thereafter he was always looked at somewhat askance by proper Philadelphians. And there had been other discouragements: lack of portrait commissions, and of sales of his other pictures, even his genre subjects.

All these factors explain a change in his art in middle life. His early work had shown an involvement in the contemporary scene, outdoor activities and community life, and even a tentative step toward imaginative themes. But after the middle 1880's, when he had turned forty, he abandoned these broader subjects, except occasionally, and devoted himself almost entirely to portraiture. Turning away from the outside world, he concentrated on the individual. Not that he withdrew from society; he continued to lead a normal social life, with many friends and students. In his art, humanity remained the center of interest. But his content was restricted to a narrower range.

In this more limited field he attained an increasing mastery. He was never a worldly success, and his sitters were mostly friends, pupils, or people who attracted him by their qualities of mind and character—scientists, physicians, churchmen, and professional workers like himself—musicians, teachers and fellow artists. The wealthy and fashionable were conspicuous by their absence. To him, a man's work was essential, and he liked to show him engaged in it. Dr. Gross and Dr. Agnew were pictured not in the elegance of academic robes, like Sargent's *Four Doctors,* but in the operating theater, scalpel in hand, talking to their students. This was a more authentic kind of portraiture than the conspicuous leisure favored by most portraitists.

The apparatus of the sitter's profession often played an important role. The pioneer physicist Henry A. Rowland is in his laboratory, his assistant working in the background, he himself holding one of his diffraction gratings reflecting the spectrum; while the frame, built and carved by the painter, is in his words "ornamented with lines of the spectrum and with coefficients and mathematical formulae relating to light and electricity, all original with Professor Rowland and selected by himself." Mrs. Frishmuth, collector of musical instruments, sits surrounded by instruments from every country and age, of every shape and material. Such relevant objects not only complete the portrayal of the individual, but add to the complexity and richness of the design.

The most ambitious work of Eakins' middle years was *The Agnew Clinic.* Dr. Agnew, famous surgeon and anatomist, was about to retire in 1889 as professor of surgery at the University of Pennsylvania, and his students commissioned the portrait, for $750. Instead of a conventional single figure, the artist's admiration for the doctor led him to paint his largest composition. The general conception is like that of *The Gross Clinic,* but this is a different age; Dr. Gross' dark frock coat has been replaced by the antiseptic white of modern surgery. The composition is not the centered pyramidal form of the earlier painting, but asymmetrical; the patient, the assistants and the nurse form one group, and the surgeon stands by himself; the two are connected by the curving line of the rail, in a horizontal frieze-like design. Although Agnew is not in the geometrical center, his fine head (one of Eakins' most powerful plastic creations) dominates the whole space, and becomes the dynamic focal point of the design.

The public reception of the picture was like that of *The Gross Clinic.* In conservative Philadelphia art circles it created a scandal, no doubt intensified by the fact that the patient was a woman, and the operation was for cancer of the breast. When the artists' jury of the Pennsylvania Academy invited it for the 1891 annual exhibition, the directors refused to let them hang it.

The only art organization that Eakins had ever joined, the Society of American Artists, since its liberal beginnings had grown more and more like its rival the National Academy. For several years its juries had rejected his entries, the final blow being when they refused *The Agnew Clinic* in 1892. Eakins wrote the Society: "I desire to sever all connection with the Society of American Artists. . . . For the last three years my paintings have been rejected by you, one of them the Agnew portrait, a composition more important than any I have ever seen upon your walls. . . . While in my opinion there are qualities in my work which entitle it to rank with the best in your Society, your Society's opinion must be that it ranks below much that I consider frivolous and superficial. These opinions are irreconcilable."

ONE SPECIAL and seemingly paradoxical type of Eakins' portraiture was that of the Catholic clergy. Paradoxical because his family background was Protestant and Quaker, and he himself was an agnostic. His painting of the *Crucifixion* was exceptional, motivated partly by rivalry of the old masters (it has interesting similarities to Ribera's *Martyrdom of Saint Bartholomew* in the Prado) but still more by his naturalism; he said that he had never seen a painting of the crucifixion in which the body was really hanging or seemed to be in the open air. It is hard to detect any positive religious feeling in the picture.

As early as 1877 Eakins had painted his first portrait of a churchman, the large canvas of Archbishop James Frederick Wood, whom he knew and asked to sit for him. But it was not until 1900 that the series commenced. Largely through Samuel Murray, who was a Catholic, he had made many good friends among the high-ranking clergy. He was attracted by their scholarship, the traditional beauty of their vestments, and the fact that many of them were Irish or Italian—two peoples for whom he had a special liking. On Sundays he and Murray used to bicycle out to St. Charles Seminary at Overbrook to spend the day. His portraits of prelates, many of high rank, all done at his request, include some of his most important works. He had kept up his Latin, and with their help he delighted in composing long Latin inscriptions for the backs of his portraits, not only of clerics but of scientists.

AS A PORTRAITIST, Eakins was concerned above all with character. The basic form of the head, its bone structure, the unique personality of the features, the character shown in hands, the shapes of the body beneath the clothes—all the factors that made the sitter an individual like no one else in the world—he grasped with unerring sureness. In this relentless search he disregarded the charm of youth, the attraction of fashion, and conventional ideas of beauty. No one ever emerged from under his brush handsomer than he or she was. Like Rembrandt, he loved old age, the marks of years and experience, the essential character that youth conceals but age reveals. Sometimes he made his sitters older and less attractive then they were. The ordinary requirements of portraiture gave way to his passion for plastic form—an urge of which he was probably not conscious, for when criticized he would say, "That's the way it was." Like all creative artists, even the most realistic, he took liberties with actualities.

The usual complaint about his portraits was their lack of "sympathy." But he was neither unsympathetic nor sentimental. Consciously he was absorbed in recording the physical reality of the individual human being, but his realization went deeper, capturing that essential element that can only be described as life. His men and women are alive; beautiful or homely, they exist. They are pictured with a depth of insight, an inner life, a feeling for their basic humanity, that make most portraitists seem superficial.

In American art this was the age of the American Woman, when academic painters were more preoccupied with women than ever before in our history, and more idealistic in picturing them. By contrast, Eakins' women, while never glamorized, have a flesh-and-blood vitality and a sense of sex. They are pictured with a feeling for their individu-ality and a psychological penetration that make his portraits of them among his finest works. In a way quite different from Gilbert Stuart's charm or Sargent's sense of fashion, he can be called particularly an interpreter of women. Yet no portraitist presented a more masculine view of the male and his world. Taken as a whole, Eakins' portraiture is the most mature pictorial record of the American people of his time—equal to Copley's record of Colonial America.

Most of his portraits by their nature were less complex in design than his earlier outdoor and figure subjects. But his larger, more ambitious portraits showed an in-creased command of a different type of design. Everything was on a larger scale. The forms were seen more broadly and handled more freely, with a richer plastic sense. The composition was often enriched by accessories, but they were subordinated and finely related to the central motif, the figure, whose sculptural forms dominated the whole. Particularly in the head was concentrated a vitality of form so intense that it seemed to fill all the space around it. Few portraitists have shown such a realization of the human head as one of the most magnetic forms in nature. In the finest of his mature portraits Eakins achieved mastery of a personal kind of design, whose strength lay not in com-plexity or movement, but in central elements realized with maximum substance and intensity—design of simplified, concentrated, monumental power.

But none of these qualities were calculated to make him a popular portraitist. The average sitter does not care for purely artistic qualities, nor for too much character. The usual function of a portrait is to please the sitter when he is alive and remind his family agreeably of him after he is gone. But Eakins' portraits were not like that; they were not intended to please anybody, they were not necessarily nice for the family to have around. They were something more important—works of art, meant primarily to satisfy the artist, but satisfying also to those who appreciate truth, character, and superb painting.

Commissions were rare. Almost all his portraits were labors of love; he asked the sitters to pose, and afterwards gave them the pictures. Even so, they often did not bother to take them away, or sometimes destroyed, or conveniently lost them. His canvases accumulated until he had a studio full of them.

A different kind of sitter was Walt Whitman, living in Camden across the Delaware River. Eakins admired Whitman, and the poet responded in kind, preferring Eakins' portrait to any other. "I never knew but one artist, and that's Tom Eakins," he said, "who could resist the temptation to see what they thought ought to be rather than what is." Again, comparing the picture to John W. Alexander's skillful idealization, "Eakins is not a painter, he is a force."

IN THE AMERICAN art world, from the late 1880's, Eakins' reputation waned. The prevailing tendencies—impressionist absorption in outdoor light, color and appearances, the brilliant visual naturalism of the Sargent school, and Whistler's decorative aestheticism—were against everything he stood for. Whereas in youth he had faced hostility, he now suffered the worse fate of neglect—a neglect more complete than any major artist in our history. His pictures were exhibited less widely (chiefly at the Pennsylvania Academy); he had no dealer in New York, never had a one-man show there, and only one in Philadelphia; until 1901 he received only three unimportant prizes; and not a single article was published on his work during his lifetime. The few sales were for low figures, usually a few hundred dollars; only two or three times did he receive over a thousand. In later years he seems to have given up any hope of making his living by art. After his father's death in 1899, however, he had a small independent income.

But he never lost his awareness of his own merit, or his enjoyment of painting. Not only did he keep on working in the same uncompromising realistic style, but in the last decade of his active career he painted twice as many pictures as in any corresponding period, including some of his strongest works, such as *The Thinker, Mrs. Frishmuth, Professor Miller, Professor Forbes,* the later versions of the William Rush theme, and most of his Catholic portraits.

Yet there can be no doubt that the wall of indifference that surrounded him had an effect. Those who knew him best in later years spoke of sadness and disillusionment. One can see this in his self-portrait painted for the National Academy when he was approaching sixty. But one can also see strength, courage and ironic humor.

Nevertheless, there can be little doubt that his art was affected by the hostility toward him as artist and teacher in early manhood, and the lack of recognition in later years. Any artist, no matter how strong, is in some degree influenced by his relations with the society of which he is a part. If he is a realist like Eakins, drawing his material from that society, the lack of response can be injurious. His early work had been that of a man who felt himself part of his community, and portrayed it from many aspects, in a deeply affirmative spirit. One cannot but regret his giving up the broader subject matter of those early years, and in particular, his virtual abandonment of figure painting except in the form of portraiture. It is true that he extended the portrait far beyond its usual limits, creating works which in both their human and plastic qualities were not only among his strongest, but among the strongest artistic creations of nineteenth-century America. But portraiture, great as he made it, did not offer the full sensuous and plastic possibilities of which he was capable. In his few paintings in which the nude or semi-nude figure had played a part, he had attained his greatest freedom and fullest develop-

Portrait of a Lady with a Setter Dog
c. 1885. Oil. 30 x 23
The Metropolitan Museum of Art

Miss Amelia C. Van Buren
c. 1889-91. Oil. 45 x 32
The Phillips Collection

ment of design. If he had painted more such themes he might have more often achieved, in addition to the concentrated power of his portraits, a plastic completeness beyond any American contemporary—except his exact opposite in most respects, Albert Ryder. As it was, the fundamental sensuousness of his art too seldom reached full expression. The limitations of the world in which he lived, together with his own realistic limitations, prevented full realization of his potentialities.

But to say this is also to recognize the extent of those potentialities, and the degree to which he did realize them. With all these qualifications, Eakins' achievement was monumental. He was our first major painter of the nineteenth century to accept completely the realities of American life, and out of them to create a profound and powerful art.

WITH THE OPENING of the new century he began to receive a measure of recognition. In 1902 the National Academy finally elected him an associate, and two months later a full academician. The Carnegie Institute in Pittsburgh invited him to show in all their international exhibitions from 1896 on, and he served on their jury of awards for five consecutive shows. There was a flurry of prizes. A strange recognition was the purchase in 1914 by Dr. Albert C. Barnes of a study for the Agnew portrait, for about four thousand dollars—three times as much as he had ever been paid. This was news, and reporters called at the quiet house on Mount Vernon Street to interview "the dean of American painters." To a request for his opinion on "the present and future of American art," he said: "If America is to produce great painters and if young art students wish to assume a place in the history of the art of their country, their first desire should be to remain in America, to peer deeper into the heart of American life, rather than to spend their time abroad obtaining a superficial view of the art of the Old World. In the days when I studied abroad conditions were entirely different. The facilities for study in this country were meager. There were even no life classes in our art schools. . . . Of course, it is well to go abroad and see the works of the old masters, but Americans must branch out into their own field, as they are doing. They must strike out for themselves, and only by doing this will we create a great and distinctly American art."

In 1910 his robust health began to decline, and after this he painted hardly at all. On June 25, 1916, he died in the house in which he had lived almost all his life.

EAKINS' ART, like Ryder's, and to some extent Homer's, was independent of contemporary European movements, and indeed counter to them. All three were anachronistic in relation to international trends, which were evolving from impressionism through post-impressionism to fauvism and the other modern movements. It seems paradoxical that these three, who to us seem more contemporary than any other Americans of their time, were so little involved in world tendencies. But this had been true of some of the most original American artists of the nineteenth century. In a nation so relatively young, our artists had to assimilate a new world which had been little used as raw material for art. There was no long native tradition out of which they could develop. They were on their own, drawing their content from American life or the inner life of the mind, and speaking in their own style. Hence our most original creative artists of the nineteenth century, while strong in individual character, played little part in the innovating international movements of their time. Such innovations came mostly from Europe, transmitted by less creative and more impressionable personalities. Through the interaction of these two forces—native creativity, the root of the whole tree, and the fertilizing influences of world art—American art grew toward maturity. The qualities that endure are not necessarily in accord with the surface currents of a period, but with the deeper currents of individual and national character.

Between Rounds
1899. Oil. 50¼ x 40
Philadelphia Museum of Art

William Rush Carving His Allegorical Figure of the Schuylkill River
1908. Oil. 36 x 47¾
The Brooklyn Museum

ABOVE
Nude Woman Seated, Wearing a Mask
Probably c. 1866. Charcoal. 24 x 18
Philadelphia Museum of Art

Home Scene
Probably late 1870 or 1871. Oil. 22 x 18¼
The Brooklyn Museum

The Biglin Brothers Turning the Stake
1873. Oil. $40\frac{1}{4}$ x $60\frac{1}{4}$
The Cleveland Museum of Art

Starting Out After Rail
1874. Oil. 24 x 20
Museum of Fine Arts, Boston

OPPOSITE
Baby at Play
1876. Oil. 32¼ x 48
Collection of Mr. and Mrs. John Hay Whitney

The Chess Players
1876. Oil. 11¾ x 16¾
The Metropolitan Museum of Art

Mrs. John H. Brinton
1878. Oil. 24¼ x 20⅛
Collection of Mrs. Rodolphe Meyer de Schauensee

Negro Boy Dancing
1878. Watercolor. 18⅛ x 22⅝
The Metropolitan Museum of Art

Spinning
1881. Watercolor. 11 x 8 (sight)
Mrs. John Randolph Garrett, Sr.

Mending the Net
1881. Oil. 32¼ x 45¼
Philadelphia Museum of Art

OPPOSITE
The Fairman Rogers Four-in-hand
1879. Oil. 24 x 36
Philadelphia Museum of Art

Shad-fishing at Gloucester on the Delaware River
1881. Oil. 12⅛ x 18¼
Philadelphia Museum of Art

OPPOSITE
The Pathetic Song
1881. Oil. 45 x 32½
The Corcoran Gallery of Art

The Agnew Clinic. Detail, Head of Dr. Agnew

OPPOSITE
The Agnew Clinic
1889. Oil. 74½ x 130½
University of Pennsylvania, School of Medicine

Professor Henry A. Rowland
Probably 1897. Oil. 82½ x 53¾
Addison Gallery of American Art, Phillips Academy

The Concert Singer
1892. Oil. 75 x 54
Philadelphia Museum of Art

Maud Cook
1895. Oil. 24 x 20
Yale University Art Gallery

OPPOSITE
Mrs. Letitia Wilson Jordan Bacon
1888. Oil. 60 x 40
The Brooklyn Museum

William H. Macdowell
c. 1891. Oil. 28 x 22
Randolph-Macon Woman's College

OPPOSITE
Salutat
1898. Oil. 49½ x 39½
Addison Gallery of American Art, Phillips Academy

Mrs. Samuel Murray
c. 1897. Oil. 40 x 30
F. M. Hall Collection, University of Nebraska Art Galleries

Mrs. Thomas Eakins
c. 1899. Oil. 20 x 16
The Joseph H. Hirshhorn Collection

The Thinker
1900. Oil. 82 x 42
The Metropolitan Museum of Art

OPPOSITE
Mrs. William D. Frishmuth
1900. Oil. 97 x 72½
Philadelphia Museum of Art

The Very Reverend James P. Turner
c. 1900. Oil. 24 x 20
St. Charles Borromeo Seminary

OPPOSITE
Signora Gomez d'Arza
1902. Oil. 30 x 24
The Metropolitan Museum of Art

67 *General E. Burd Grubb.* c. 1898. 30 x 22. Lent by Mrs. Reginald Marsh. G-302.

68 *Salutat.* 1898. 49½ x 39½. Lent by the Addison Gallery of American Art, Phillips Academy, Andover, Mass. G-310. Ill. p. 55.

69 *Study for "Salutat".* Probably 1898. 20 x 16. Lent by Mr. and Mrs. James H. Beal. G-311.

70 *Between Rounds.* 1899. 50¼ x 40. Lent by the Philadelphia Museum of Art. G-312. Ill. p. 34.

71 *Benjamin Eakins.* c. 1899. 24 x 20. Lent by the Philadelphia Museum of Art. G-324.

72 *Mrs. Thomas Eakins.* c. 1899. 20 x 16. Lent by the Joseph H. Hirshhorn Collection. G-325. Ill. p. 57.

73 *Mrs. William H. Green.* 1899. 27 x 22. Lent by the Joseph H. Hirshhorn Collection. G-326.

74 *The Dean's Roll Call.* 1899. 84 x 42. Lent by the Museum of Fine Arts, Boston, Abraham Shuman Fund. G-327.

75 *William M. Chase.* c. 1899. 24 x 20. Lent by the Joseph H. Hirshhorn Collection. G-330.

76 *The Thinker.* 1900. 82 x 42. Lent by The Metropolitan Museum of Art, Kennedy Fund, 1917. G-331. Ill. p. 58.

77 *Addie.* 1900. 24⅛ x 18¼. Lent by the Philadelphia Museum of Art. G-333.

78 *Robert M. Lindsay.* 1900. 24 x 20. Lent by The Detroit Institute of Arts, Gift of Dexter M. Ferry, Jr. G-335.

79 *Frank Jay St. John.* 1900. 23½ x 19. Private Collection, New York. G-337.

80 *Mrs. William D. Frishmuth.* 1900. 97 x 72½. Lent by the Philadelphia Museum of Art. G-338. Ill. p. 59.

81 *Mrs. Joseph H. Drexel.* 1900. 47 x 37. Lent by the Joseph H. Hirshhorn Collection. G-339.

82 *The Very Reverend James P. Turner.* c. 1900. 24 x 20. Lent by St. Charles Borromeo Seminary. G-347. Ill. p. 60.

83 *Professor Leslie W. Miller.* 1901. 88⅛ x 43¼. Lent by the Philadelphia Museum of Art. G-348.

84 *Self-portrait.* 1902. 30 x 25. Lent by the National Academy of Design. G-358.

85 *Signora Gomez d'Arza.* 1902. 30 x 24. Lent by The Metropolitan Museum of Art, George A. Hearn Fund, 1927. G-360. Ill. p. 61.

86 *Sebastiano Cardinal Martinelli.* 1902. 79¼ x 60. Lent by The Armand Hammer Foundation. G-361.

87 *The Very Reverend John J. Fedigan.* 1902. 89½ x 50. Lent by Villanova University. G-362.

88 *The Translator—The Right Reverend Hugh Thomas Henry.* 1902. 50 x 40. Lent by St. Charles Borromeo Seminary. G-364.

89 *The Right Reverend James F. Loughlin.* 1902. 90 x 45. Lent by St. Charles Borromeo Seminary. G-365.

90 *William B. Kurtz.* 1903. 52 x 32. Private Collection. G-378.

91 *Music.* 1904. 39⅜ x 49½. Lent by the Albright-Knox Art Gallery. G-402. Ill. p. 62.

92 *Frank B. A. Linton.* 1904. 24 x 20. Lent by the Joseph H. Hirshhorn Collection. G-406.

93 *William H. Macdowell.* c. 1904. 24 x 20. Lent by the Memorial Art Gallery of the University of Rochester. G-416.

94 *Professor William Smith Forbes.* 1905. 84 x 48. Lent by the Jefferson Medical College of Philadelphia. G-422.

95 *Monsignor Diomede Falconio.* 1905. 72⅛ x 54¼. Lent by the National Gallery of Art, Washington, D. C., Gift of Stephen C. Clark. G-425. Ill. p. 64.

96 *A. W. Lee.* 1905. 40 x 32. Lent by Reynolda House. G-427. Ill. p. 65.

97 *Miss Elizabeth L. Burton.* 1906. 30 x 25. Lent by The Minneapolis Institute of Arts. G-428.

98 *William Rush Carving His Allegorical Figure of the Schuylkill River.* 1908. 36 x 47¾. Lent by The Brooklyn Museum. G-445. Ill. p. 35.

99 *William Rush and His Model.* 1908. 35¼ x 47¼. Lent by the Honolulu Academy of Arts. G-451. Ill. p. 63.

100 *William Rush's Model.* 1908. 36 x 23½. Lent by Mr. and Mrs. Sheldon Keck. G-453.

101 *The Old-fashioned Dress.* c. 1908. 60⅜ x 40¼. Lent by the Philadelphia Museum of Art. G-457.

102 *The Old-fashioned Dress (Study).* c. 1908. 36 x 22. Private Collection. G-459.

103 *Dr. Edward Anthony Spitzka.* c. 1913. 30 x 25. Lent by the Joseph H. Hirshhorn Collection. G-474.

104 *Studies for "William Rush Carving his Allegorical Figure of the Schuylkill River."* 1877. Bronze. Head of Rush, 7¼ high. Washington, 8⅛ high. Nymph and Bittern, 9¼ high. Lent by Seymour Adelman. G-498, a, c and d.

105 *Spinning.* 1882-83. Bronze. 18 x 14½. Lent by the Pennsylvania Academy of the Fine Arts. G-504.

106 *Knitting.* 1882–83. Bronze. 18 x 15. Lent by the Pennsylvania Academy of the Fine Arts. G-505.

107 *Arcadia.* 1883. Bronze. 12½ x 25. Lent by James Wyeth. G-506.

108 *The American Army Crossing the Delaware.* 1893. Bronze. 55 x 94. Lent by the Joseph H. Hirshhorn Foundation. G-513. Ill. p. 66.

109 *The Battle of Trenton.* 1893. Bronze. 55 x 94. Lent by the Joseph H. Hirshhorn Foundation. G-514. Ill. p. 67.

Numbers 110-133 are photographs by Eakins, except 113. All except 131 are lent by The Metropolitan Museum of Art; of these, 111-113 and 115-121 were purchases from the David Hunter McAlpin Fund, 1943; 110, 114, 122-130, 132 and 133 were Gifts of Charles Bregler, 1941, 1944 and 1961.

110 *William H. Macdowell and Margaret Eakins at Saltville, Virginia.* c. 1881. 10⅞ x 7⅞.

111 *Two Girls in Greek Dress beside a Plaster Cast of Eakins' "Arcadia."* c. 1883. 14 x 10 1/16.

112 *J. Laurie Wallace Playing Pipes.* c. 1883. 9 x 6⅞.

113 *Thomas Eakins.* (Probably by J. Laurie Wallace.) c. 1883. 9 x 6½.

114 *Eakins' Students Boxing.* Probably early 1880's. 8 x 10.

115 *Seated Male Nude.* 9¼ x 8⅝.

116 *Female Model, Reclining.* 2 13/16 x 5¼.

117 *Female Model, Reclining.* 4½ x 6.

118 *Female Model, Seated.* 7 x 8½.

119 *George W. Holmes.* 10 7/16 x 8 1/16.

120 *William H. Macdowell, Eakins' Father-in-law.* 7 11/16 x 5 11/16.

121 *William H. Macdowell.* 5 11/16 x 6 9/16.

122 *Mrs. William H. Macdowell.* 9 15/16 x 8.

123 *Multiple Exposure Photograph: Jesse Godley Running.* 1884/5. 8 x 10.

124 *Multiple Exposure Photograph: Man Walking.* 1884/5. 6⅞ x 8⅞.

125 to 130 *Six Multiple Exposure Photographs: Men Jumping, Walking, Pole-vaulting; A Woman Walking.* 1884/5. Each 3¾ x 4¾.

131 *Multiple Exposure Photograph: Boy Jumping.* 1884/5. 11⅛ x 14. Enlargement from negative owned by the Franklin Institute, Philadelphia.

132 *Cowboy at B. T. Ranch, Dakota.* 1887. 9 15/16 x 8 1/16.

133 *The William J. Crowell Family at Avondale, Pennsylvania.* Probably 1890. 9⅞ x 13 9/16.